Original title:
Elderflower Elegy

Copyright © 2025 Creative Arts Management OÜ
All rights reserved.

Author: Hugo Fitzgerald
ISBN HARDBACK: 978-1-80567-002-5
ISBN PAPERBACK: 978-1-80567-082-7

## Reflections in Petal Rain

In a field where daisies dance and spin,
A bee forgot to wear a hat and grin.
It buzzed in circles, tripped over a bloom,
Declaring nectar was its only groom.

"Oh look at me!" the buttercup did shout,
"I'm the fairest, no room for doubt!"
While petals rained like confetti in June,
The daisies swayed to nature's silly tune.

## An Elegy in the Meadow

In fields of dreams, where grass does play,
A hedgehog danced, then rolled away.
He tripped on roots and tumbled in glee,
Squeaking softly, "Oh why is this me?"

The daisies snickered, oh what a sight,
As he sported twigs, his chosen delight.
With laughter echoing through warm, sweet air,
Life's a funny ballet, if you dare!

## The Lament of Blossom's Bane

A robin perched with crumbs in its beak,
Whispered tales of the blooms, so bleak.
"Why can't they see, I'm the star today?"
While petals sighed, "We must go away!"

From the branches came giggles, soft and sly,
As squirrels tossed acorns, oh me, oh my!
The flowers wobbled in the gentle breeze,
Wondering if they could dance with ease.

## Dappled Light and Dying Fragrance

In dappled light where shadows play,
A butterfly had lost its way.
It flapped and floundered, a comic sight,
Stumbling over petals, not quite right.

A fragrant odor filled the bright day,
"Do I smell like cheese?" it puffed in dismay.
While blooms just chuckled, sharing their grace,
Beauty's absurdity is part of the race.

## When the Blossoms Weep

When blooms begin to droop and sigh,
The bees just buzz, they can't comply.
They bumble forth with tipsy cheer,
While petals fall like sneaky tears.

Oh, laughter sprouts where sorrow strains,
As petals chase away the pains.
With giggles caught in winds of fate,
These blossoms laugh and tease our fate.

## Memories Woven in White

In gardens bright with fuzzy bees,
We spun our tales beneath the trees.
With every joke and foolish grin,
We wove our joys, let giggles spin.

The flowers winked, their petals talk,
As laughter danced—a lovely clock.
Each white bloom knows a secret well,
A tale of mischief it will tell.

## A Cup of Mournful Tea

I brewed a cup of flowery dreams,
With sips of sunshine, or so it seems.
Yet every drop brings chuckles near,
As silly thoughts begin to steer.

Each leaf a shriek, each steep a jest,
As warmth combines with comical zest.
Though mourning's mask might paint the scene,
My cup of tea stays humor's queen.

## Crumpled Leaves and Old Songs

With crumpled leaves beneath our feet,
We danced around to silly beats.
Old songs of sweetness fill the air,
As laughter lifts our spirits fair.

Each rustled page, a tale so bright,
The leaves jump up in sheer delight.
When joy's the tune, we all can sing,
And every crumple starts to swing.

## Nectar of Nostalgia

In the garden, bees do buzz,
Chasing sweetness just because.
Forgotten laughs in air so thick,
With memories that gently stick.

Sipping nectar, oh what glee,
Honey, lavender, and a tree.
Did we trample blooms in our chase?
Amidst the chaos, we found our place.

Early mornings, sleepyhead,
Stumbling out of our bed.
A toast to petals, wild and free,
Yet, watch your step, oh silly me!

And though those flowers fade away,
Their laughter lingers, come what may.
In every sip, a tale retold,
Of summers vibrant, brave, and bold.

## Wandering through White Blossoms

White clouds tumble, petals drift,
In this maze, I lose my gift.
Wandering through the glorious bloom,
I think I've found a witch's room!

The scent it tickles, nose and mind,
A floral joke, how unrefined.
What's that? A bee in my hair?
A buzzing buzzard, should I care?

Rumbling stomach, that's my plight,
Did I sample too many bites?
Each flower whispers, 'Not too sweet!'
Like my cousin Steve, on repeat.

So here I am, twirling around,
In bewilderment, joy is found.
With comical grace, I finally spring,
Waltzing along with the bee on wing.

## The Garden's Quiet Song

In quiet corners, giggles grow,
Each trembling leaf holds tales to sow.
The garden hums a gentle tune,
With flowers dancing by the moon.

But watch your step, oh what a sight,
I tripped over a bush last night!
With petals flying, laughter soared,
While critters watched, entirely bored.

The hedgehog snickered, called me slow,
As I fell down with quite a show.
"Oh what elegance!" they would tease,
In blossoms' grace, I found my ease.

Yet still I wander, mischief's muse,
Unruly roads, I simply choose.
Each floral note a quirky fling,
In this soft garden, I hear them sing.

**Fading Fragrance**

Once fragrant blooms now start to fade,
Like my attempts at being suave.
Last week's party, quite the affair,
And I spilled punch everywhere!

Those fragrant whispers call my name,
Recalling odd mishaps of fame.
Did I really wear that hat?
While grinning like a garden brat?

The vinaigrette, a skyward spray,
The picnic scuffles, fashion's play.
With every scent, a tale unfolds,
Of friendship wrapped in marigolds.

So as the flowers bid goodnight,
I start to giggle, what a sight!
In memories sweet, I find my cheer,
A fading fragrance, oh so dear.

## **Pastel Days and Silver Nights**

In gardens bright with pastel hues,
The bees wear tiny, silly shoes.
They dance on blooms, a clumsy feat,
As petals giggle under their feet.

With silver moonlight, we all convene,
To sip the nectar, oh so keen.
Yet every sip brings a floral sneeze,
And laughter echoes through the trees.

Oh, what joy in these silly days,
With gusty winds that twist and sway.
We wear the pollen in our hair,
And prance like fairies without a care.

So raise a glass to joys so right,
In pastel days and silver nights!
Where flowers laugh and spirits bloom,
And joy escapes like sweet perfume.

## The Fable of Flowers Unsung

Once blooms gathered for a scheme,
To craft a tale, or so it seemed.
The daisies claimed they were the best,
While roses puffed with floral zest.

A tulip chimed in, quite absurd,
"I'm the star; you're all unheard!"
But every bud had much to say,
Until the wind blew them away.

A bumblebee, with sticky paws,
Swore he would help, but then he snores.
The petals sighed, their chance now gone,
As sunlit hours slipped to dawn.

So heed this fable, oh dear friends,
Even flowers need help to mend.
For in the laughter of the bees,
Their unsung tales take flight in breeze.

## Sorrowful Sips of Spring

In springtime's cheer, we sip with glee,
Yet every gulp feels like a spree.
A vine-wrapped cup, a twist of taste,
That leaves us feeling quite misplaced.

With straws like daisies, we all slurp,
And giggles come with every burp.
"Oops, excuse me!" is the common refrain,
As flower crowns begin to wane.

The willow weeps, or so it seems,
As we share our springtime dreams.
With every sip, a petal drops,
And soon we're on our funny hops.

So let's toast to those flubbed delights,
In sorrowful sips of silly nights!
For laughter blooms where friends unite,
In cups of joy, we take flight.

## When Blossoms Bow

When blossoms bow from summer's heat,
They form a line, a floral greet.
With petals straighter than a rod,
They put on shows that seem quite odd.

The sunflowers spin, a whirlwind dance,
While violets giggle, lost in trance.
They twirl and leap, as breezes flute,
Creating chaos, oh what a hoot!

A dandelion, trivial and bright,
Wants to join in, with all its might.
But sneezes fly, and petals scatter,
In the merry madness, what's the matter?

So when blossoms bow, take a glance,
For nature's humor is worth a chance!
In every slip and every spin,
Lies the joy of where we've been.

## Petals Through Time

In a garden of laughter, petals dance,
Golden echoes of a leafy romance.
A bee with a bow tie, buzzing with flair,
Sips nectar like prosecco, without a care.

Tickling blooms in a silly parade,
Whispers of secrets that flowers have made.
Dewdrops like giggles, rolling down leaves,
Nature's own comedy, oh how it believes!

With petals a-wobble, they cha-cha away,
And daisies in spectacles come out to play.
The sun laughs aloud, tickling the trees,
As squirrels juggle acorns, imagining tea.

So let's toast to blooms that never say die,
With sprigs of wild humor that tickle the sky.
In this garden of jokes, there's not one frown,
Just petals and punchlines spreading around!

## **Floral Compositions**

A bouquet of giggles, in vases reside,
With roses that whisper, and tulips employed.
Lilies, they trumpet, with outrageous delight,
While orchids perform in a velvety light.

In this symphony sweet, blooms play their part,
Daffodils dancing, invoking the heart.
Marigolds, too, with a cheeky grin,
Spread rhymes in the air, where the fun begins.

Petals of color, like notes on a staff,
Compose laughter, with every soft laugh.
Sunflowers waltz, just as bees play a tune,
And daisies debate who's the fairest of June.

So let's mix our bouquets, a riot of cheer,
With twirls and with whirls, let's get the crowd near.
As nature composes this jovial dream,
We'll laugh with the flowers, as friends in a team!

## Heartstrings of a Fading Bloom

Oh, heartstrings of blooms, we all find quite funny,
When roses start blushing, and daisies look sunny.
The violets giggle, saying, "We're next!"
While dahlias take selfies, looking perplexed.

Petals in twilight take one final bow,
With a wink to the sun, to the moon, and the wow!
What's this? A lilac, in fit of ballet,
Twirling at dusk, like it's heading to play.

A farewell so wobbly, yet a humor so bright,
As dusk blends the colors, making the night.
With heartstrings of laughter, they sing through the gloom,
Each fading petal, a laugh with a zoom.

So raise a glass high for our fragile friends,
Who wink at the heavens and giggle as end.
For every bloom fades, but the chuckles remain,
In a garden of memories, where joy knows no chain.

## Last Call of the Garden

Last call for the blooms, before night takes its stage,
The petals convene, in a leafy old age.
"Who's got the punchline?" the daisies all shout,
"Let's laugh at the world, while we twirl all about!"

The peonies snicker, with a wink of their bloom,
As tulips proclaim they'll humor the gloom.
They gather in circles, like friends at a bar,
With whispered delights, full of giggles to spar.

The wind carries tales of the floral brigade,
As colors fade gently, yet joy won't evade.
"For tomorrow, the sunlight will offer us cheer,
So let's dance, my dear petals, with no room for fear!"

So here's to the last call, with laughter in tow,
To the blooms and their antics, their delightful show.
As the night takes the crown, may the joy take a flight,
In our garden of giggles, we'll be alright!

## The Lament of Lost Petals

In the garden, petals lay,
Once so bright, now gone astray.
Bumblebees now search in vain,
Grumbling softly, feeling pain.

For every bloom that floats away,
A dandelion dares to play.
Wishing it could wear a crown,
Instead, it's called a weedy clown.

The squirrels laugh with cheeky grins,
While petals cry of wasted spins.
When rains arrive and skies turn gray,
They join the dance of the dismay.

So raise a glass to petals lost,
Let's toast to them at any cost.
Life's a giggle, even in gloom,
Cheers to the flowers in full bloom!

# Frosted Tips of Seasonal Remembrance

In winter's grasp, the flowers freeze,
Like frosted tips of perfumed tease.
They wish for sun, a gentle cheer,
But find themselves wrapped up in fear.

Each daisy shivers, hugs the ground,
While frosty whispers swirl around.
"Let's not forget our sunny days!"
The petals shout in humorous ways.

A lilac dreams of summer's heat,
Yet finds a snowflake on its seat.
It quips, "What's this, a frosty joke?"
As icy winds make laughter choke.

Though frost may dim their vibrant cheer,
Each bloom giggles, "We'll persevere!"
For every chill that fills the air,
Floral humor, beyond compare!

## In the Presence of Fading Beauty

Once a bloom of splendid sight,
Now a shadow, what a fright!
Petals droop and cheeks turn brown,
Is this what they mean by 'let down'?

The violet sighs, "Oh, where's my hue?"
While roses reminisce, too.
"Once I had a glorious stand,
Now I'm just a wilted brand."

The daisies giggle, bright and bold,
"Fading's not so bad, we're told.
Let's throw a party for our fate,
And celebrate our wrinkles' rate!"

So under moonlight, they convene,
Fading beauty, far from serene.
With laughter shared, they find a way,
To turn decay into bouquet play!

## Silent Reverie of the Garden

In the garden, whispers flow,
Petals gossip, 'neath the snow.
"A bouquet's lost its former style,
Where are the peonies, all the while?"

The marigolds, with faces bright,
Try to cheer up the muted sight.
"Let's make a joke of winter's sting,
And have a laugh while robins sing!"

Amidst the blooms that frown with glee,
The tulips declare, "Just let it be!"
For every petal that fades away,
Laughter's left to gently sway.

So raise a cheer for all we've lost,
Each wilted petal, worth the cost.
In silent reverie, they still sing,
Funny flowers, our hearts they bring!

**The Melancholy of Wildflowers**

In a field of yellow blooms,
The bees start to hum in tune,
Yet petals drop with a funny flop,
As if they're dancing to an offbeat swoon.

The daisies wink at the pansies near,
While grasshoppers chirp with a hearty cheer,
But when the rain pours down like a joke,
Even sunflowers frown, it's a wildflower leer!

Oh, the buttercups giggle in the breeze,
While dandelions share their stories with ease,
But the wind steals a petal, oh what a plight,
A daisy's worried, "Was that my best tease?"

So let's raise a toast to blooms that sway,
With petals so bright they might just play,
At the end of the day when blooms say bye,
They'll crack a joke in an elegant way.

## Farewell to the Fragrant Dawn

Good morning to the flowers, they sing,
Sniffing the sun like it's a fine spring fling,
But all that pollen makes them sneeze,
A fragrant dawn now sounds like a ding!

The lilacs laugh with their purple hats,
While roses complain about the bees and chats,
And when the sun sets, it's really quite clear,
That every flower thinks it's all just chitchats!

The tulips pout when the dew turns cold,
Saying, "This morning warmth, oh let it unfold!"
Yet they shiver, trying to look so cool,
Their petals folded in a frosty hold.

So here's to the dawn and all its jest,
A symphony of blooms at their feathered best,
With laughter and giggles tucked in their seams,
They bid goodbye, dreaming wildflower dreams.

## Disappearing Without a Sound

In the garden of whims, they pop and fade,
Wildflowers vanish like a prankster's charade,
One moment they're there, waving in style,
Next thing you know, they're gone—how they trade!

Petals drop silently like jokes on the floor,
And everyone wonders, "What's sure to restore?"
The grasses all chuckle, oh what a crowd,
As flowers go poof, without a rapport!

The shy violets whisper a mischievous tale,
Of poppies that tripped on their own rosy trail,
They giggle as petals swirl to the ground,
It's nature's own riddle—worth more than a sale.

So let's watch and laugh at what comes and goes,
These blooms of the moment, those shy little shows,
For in this grand garden, a jest or two,
Is the essence of laughter that everyone knows.

## The Blooming Passage

Through the arch of blossoms, we wander and sway,
With flowers that giggle in a bustly ballet,
Tulips tiptoe in colors of fun,
As they pirouette gently, welcoming play.

The daisies tell tales of the bees at dawn,
While peonies blush at the cute bumble's yawn,
They all trade their secrets like gossipy friends,
Amidst petals and laughs, an unwritten spawn.

Oh, the blooming adventure in sun-dappled light,
Each flower a punchline in nature's delight,
As sunflowers beam, it's a whimsical sight,
In this passage of blooms, life's a sheer delight!

So come dance with the petals, let laughter ensue,
With every sweet fragrance, joy sprinkles through,
For in gardens where chuckles bloom as we roam,
The passage is bright, where we all find our groove.

## The Fragility of Fleeting Days

The sun peeks through the leaves, oh my!
A squirrel steals my snack and runs awry.
I chase him down, it's quite a sight,
But tripping over roots, my fate's not bright.

We laugh at time, it slips so fast,
With petals falling, summer's cast.
Yet every mishap makes me cheer,
For fleeting days, I hold so dear.

In jars of jam, we pour our thrills,
The taste of laughter gives us chills.
A dance with bees, a waltz with breeze,
Life's funny moments, oh, such tease!

So let us sip our flower tea,
And toast to life, wild and free.
With every giggle, as we say,
These fleeting days are here to stay!

## **Misty Hues of Yesteryears**

What's that smell? A memory here!
From misty days, I shed a tear.
With laughter ringing through the trees,
Those hazy hours bring me to my knees.

We wore those hats, not quite in style,
And danced like fools for quite a while.
The blossoms bloom, then quickly fade,
Oh, how I miss that silly parade.

With winds that whisper through the glade,
I recall the plays and pranks we made.
Each silly step, a perfect jest,
In yesteryears, we felt the best.

So raise a cup and share a laugh,
At memories gone—we're just half.
For every cringe we now regret,
It's all in love, don't you forget!

## The Space Between Blooms

In gardens where the giggles grow,
The flowers bloom, then start to bow.
A bumblebee approaches slow,
He steals the show—don't say hello!

The petals burst with colors bright,
Yet leave the weeds to claim the night.
We dance with joy, but please take care,
The space between blooms holds hidden fair.

I trip on vines, they use my shoe,
And laugh at me, oh, how they grew!
With every stumble, I find a rhyme,
In spaces between, I waste no time.

So let the blooms share secrets deep,
While I chase shadows, not a peep.
With every laugh, I plant a seed,
In spaces between, we'll take the lead!

## **A Canvas of Distant Echoes**

A canvas painted with fading hues,
Echoes of laughter, like soft morning news.
The brush slides down, with every stroke,
Creating memories, ripe to provoke.

I add a splash of mustard yellow,
For those silly pranks by my dear fellow.
Then splatter on some sassy red,
For every time the garden dad tread.

With petals brushed on, we can't forget,
Those echoes of fun, our happy duet.
A dance in the shade, a shout in the breeze,
Each color a laugh that's sure to please.

So let me paint, and let me cheer,
With echoes of joy that draw you near.
In every stroke, a giggle blooms,
On this canvas wide, with no more glooms!

## Whispers of the White Blossom

In a garden where daisies dance,
The flowers whisper, given a chance.
Stumbling bees in their clumsy flight,
Seek nectar sweet till the loss of light.

A cat with a hat leaps on the scene,
Chasing shadows like a sprite unseen.
Petals flutter, giggling in the air,
While gossiping roses lend an ear with flair.

Old trees chuckle, their branches sway,
As daisies debate who'll lead the play.
A rabbit in glasses reads the news,
While singing violets sip on their brews.

So here's to the blooms, a funny array,
With laughter woven in petals' display.
Life's a comedy in the garden's embrace,
Where flowers and whimsy have all found their place.

## The Scent of Soft Remembrance

A skunk in disguise, a fragrant delight,
Drifting through meadows, what a sight!
She tells tales of the blooms that pass,
And highs of the sun, as she nibbles on grass.

Whispers of perfume fill the warm air,
As floppy-eared rabbits hop everywhere.
With botanist bees in their critter coats,
Mixing potions like true herbal gnomes.

Old daisies remember a time of their youth,
When they danced with the wind and spoke the truth.
Now they're plucking gray hairs, counting a few,
While knitting sweet garlands and brewing up stew.

Charmed memories flit with a giggle and cheer,
The scent in the breeze tickles your ear.
So here's a toast to the blossoms that sway,
In a funny old world, where laughter can play.

## A Delicate Farewell

Buds in a bustle, a playful parade,
Frantic petals, in sunshine, they fade.
As clouds chuckle, tickling blooms so bright,
They wave their goodbyes before the night.

A shy little flower, in polka-dot lace,
Trip over their stems, in a clumsy grace.
They're off to the ball, the pollen-a-palooza,
Where butterflies twirl in a colorful moola.

Leaves whistle tunes, a farewell to sing,
To petals that prance with a hopeful spring.
The sun nods goodbye, with a wink and a smile,
Leaving behind a scene so worthwhile.

So laugh with the blossoms, don't shed a tear,
For in every farewell, fun memories appear.
A party of petals, making their way,
In a delicate dance, till the end of the day.

# Nectar in the Twilight

When twilight descends with a twist of glee,
The flowers convene for a tea party spree.
The violets gossip, the sunflowers boast,
About the best nectar and who liked it most.

A moonlit soirée, where petals grow bold,
The aroma of laughter is sprinkled like gold.
With fireflies buzzing and stars lending light,
The garden's a stage for this whimsical night.

The elderberries chuckle over a game,
While nightingales croon their favorite fame.
A squirrel in a tux brings the snacks with a grin,
As the daisies toast to the wild and free spin.

So sip on the nectar of joy and delight,
In the charming garden, where mischief takes flight.
For every petal that dances and sways,
Brings laughter and cheer to the end of our days.

## Nature's Final Serenade

When flowers wave their last goodbye,
A bumblebee lets out a sigh.
The petals dance in a silly breeze,
As critters collect their final fees.

The trees giggle, shedding their leaves,
While squirrels play tricks up their sleeves.
A melody of rustles and creaks,
Nature's jokes in the twilight speak.

The sun bows out with a chuckle,
As twilight's shadows start to snuggle.
The sky paints pinks with a wink and a grin,
Birds chirp laughter as day wears thin.

So let's toast to blooms that won't last,
With lemonade and a party blast!
For every end brings joy anew,
In nature's jest, we'll bid adieu!

## **A Garden's Last Goodbye**

Amidst the weeds, a gnome takes a seat,
Watching the flowers admit defeat.
As petals plummet to the ground,
The garden's giggles start to resound.

The daisies trip on their own charm,
While bees buzz in conspiratorial calm.
A tulip tips its hat in jest,
As summer's warmth puts blooms to rest.

The veggies chuckle, holding back tears,
Recalling sunshine of yesteryears.
As marigolds whisper to the vine,
It's time for this garden to unwind.

So let's raise a spade to this floral crew,
For every bloom here, there's a laugh or two.
In a patch of soil where joy resides,
Goodbyes are but jokes in thin disguise.

## **Veils of Vanishing Petals**

In the twilight, petals flutter down,
Like giggly confetti tossed all around.
They whisper sweet secrets to the ground,
With each little dive, a laugh is found.

The roses nod, all wisdom in bloom,
While daffodils dance to their own tune.
A dandelion pops, with a poof and cheer,
Blowing wishes as they disappear.

"Oh dear," sighs the lilac, "what a show!"
"I'd keep blooming if only I could grow!"
Yet laughter bubbles in the fading light,
As nature prepares for a restful night.

So let's cherish the chuckles that flowers bring,
In veils of petals, we hear them sing.
Each ending's a giggle wrapped in a sigh,
In the garden's embrace, we'll always fly.

# The Elegance of Ephemera

Once in a while, blooms burst with flair,
Outshining the clouds, with colors rare.
But time has its way of mixing the art,
And soon they pirouette with a light heart.

The poppies prance, but it's just for show,
"Catch us while you can!" they giggle below.
As the daisies yawn, they start to collapse,
Creating a scene that's full of mishaps.

Butterflies giggle, flitting in flight,
"Here today, gone tomorrow, isn't it bright?"
They twirl with the wind in a whimsical race,
Chasing each other, a comical embrace.

So let's laugh with nature, in each fading bloom,
For every bright ending, there's always room.
In the elegance of moments we hold,
Lies a playful spirit, worth more than gold.

## Soft Echoes of Summer

In clouds of white, we dance and spin,
Bees buzzing loud, they're wearing a grin.
A giggle from petals, a mischievous tease,
Summer's laughter floats on the breeze.

Frolicking blooms in the sunny light,
They play peek-a-boo, oh what a sight!
With lemonade sips and sun-kissed toes,
These mischief-makers, everybody knows.

Jars filled with charm from days gone by,
A splash of sweet grace as the minutes fly.
Whispers of frolic in every bouquet,
As we clink our glasses and shout, "Hooray!"

So raise a toast to that fragrant cheer,
To moments of joy, loud and near.
With tales of scent and laughter combined,
Summer's soft echoes, forever enshrined.

## Ghosts of Floral Days

Whispers of flowers in the soft moonlight,
They laugh and they wink; what a funny sight!
Ghostly petals with a mischievous flair,
Dancing through gardens without a care.

Oh, remember the time, we made wine from the brew?
Then tripped on the vines and fell in a stew!
The owls hooted jokes, while crickets sang low,
As we told all our secrets to the nighttime glow.

Ghoulish shadows in a floral parade,
With blooms skipping past like they're playing charades.
Each flower a jester, in glorious gowns,
While laughter erupts from the peonies' crowns.

So here's to the ghosts, our floral friends,
With stories and laughter that never ends.
In the garden where whimsy and time intertwine,
We'll sprout new tales over sips of sweet wine!

## Scented Reminiscence

A whiff of the past, what a treat it brings,
Days filled with laughter and imaginary kings.
The fizz of the bubbles from soda pop streams,
While flowers mix up our wildest dreams.

Oh, the tangled vines weave stories both bold,
Of mishaps with jam jars, and adventures retold.
Tickling our noses with sweet, cloying hue,
Scented reminiscence, how it tickles you!

Wear your floral crown with a giggly laugh,
As we float on the whimsies, just like a giraffe.
The garden is buzzing, with all of its cheer,
Planting smiles in hearts as we twirl and we cheer!

So gather the blooms in a wacky bouquet,
Let's craft a new tale for the light of day.
With each petal tossed, our hearts take flight,
In fragrant nostalgia, everything feels right.

## Time's Sweet Lament

Tick-tock on the wall, let's take a short pause,
To chuckle at moments that leave us in awe.
With sweet petaled giggles and jellybean dreams,
Time's bittersweet laughter is bursting at the seams.

Look at the daisies in a conga line,
Each sway and shimmy, so silly and fine.
While the sun plays hide-and-seek with the sky,
We'll turn back the clock with a gleeful sigh.

A sprinkle of sweetness mixed in the air,
Lemonade toast to the fun that we share.
Time drips like honey, slow but so sweet,
As we dance through the gardens, light on our feet.

So here's to the moments not quite in a rush,
ith weeds and wild laughter that make our hearts blush.

In time's sweet lament, we'll sip and we'll sway,
Relishing life in the sun's golden ray.

## Rippled Memories in the Wind

In the garden, giggles leap,
Flowers gossip secrets deep.
Bumblebees buzz like chatty friends,
Chasing joy, the laughter never ends.

Petals dance with silly grace,
Sunshine tickles every face.
Butterflies perform their quirky show,
While daisies join the rowdy flow.

Nature's whimsy paints the day,
Funny tales in bright array.
A breeze whispers "Come and play!"
As laughter flits and flies away.

## Shadows of a Softening Bloom

In twilight's glow, shadows prance,
Even roses join the dance.
A hyacinth with a wink so bright,
Claims it's the star of the night.

Laughter echoes through the glade,
Tulips tease with silly grade.
Petunias in polka dots so bold,
Spin tales of mischief, frosty and old.

Lentil beads on fern's green lace,
Mirthful whispers fill the space.
A playhouse sprung from fragrance sweet,
Where every bloom brings a tap and beat.

**Legacies of Scent**

The garden's scent, a prankster's tease,
Breezy perfume with playful ease.
Lilacs lean and wink their eyes,
While daisies whisper silly lies.

A flower crown made of jest,
In this realm, we'll never rest.
Wear it loud with laughter's might,
Crafting sprigs in pure delight.

Violets mutter, "What a show!"
As petals fall, quick as a toe.
They giggle - can you hear their jest?
In fragrant memories, we're all blessed.

## The Soliloquy of Floral Dreams

In a secret garden, dreams collide,
Where daisies have a wild ride.
Petals, like actors, play their part,
With goofy plots that touch the heart.

Sunflowers sport their jester hats,
As crickets serenade the chats.
Each morning dew's a laughter spark,
Lighting up the grassy park.

Jovial roses share a root,
While buds boast of their sweet loot.
In tales of color and soft perfume,
Life's just a lovely, silly tune.

## **Secrets Held in Petal Shade**

In gardens where the whispers play,
Petals giggle in the sunny sway.
Beneath the leaves, the tales unfold,
Of clumsy bees and nectar bold.

A waltz of blooms, a dance delight,
They spill their secrets, oh so light.
With each sweet breeze, a cheeky tease,
In rosy hues and dappled trees.

The flower folk conspire and scheme,
Over sips of honeyed dream.
They trade their stories, silly pranks,
In shades of green, they join the ranks.

So raise a cup to petals bright,
For laughter blooms in sheer delight.
With every sip we celebrate,
The merry tales of garden fate.

## Unraveling the Floral Story

Once upon a petal's sigh,
A bud mischief in the sky.
With pollen hats and tiny shoes,
The flowers laughed, shared silly news.

Whispers tangled in a breeze,
As daisies danced with such great ease.
A poppy tried to tell a joke,
But ended up a laughing folk!

The violets gossiped on the ground,
With every word, a giggle found.
A rose turned pink from all the fun,
While marigolds just blind the sun.

So gather 'round the blooming crew,
For every petal has a clue.
In nature's tales, we're free to roam,
In fragrant fields, we find our home.

## Threads of Scented Remembrance

A whiff of laughter in the air,
A floral quilt beyond compare.
With every scent, a memory twirls,
As daisies exchange their playful pearls.

In fields where jests take flight on wings,
The lavender hums while the laughter sings.
A bouquet of giggles, a twist of fate,
With rhymes of fragrance, never too late.

The violets giggle as they recall,
The time the wind made one fall.
The punctured bloom, a tale so sweet,
It tickled the petals, oh what a treat!

So cherish the moments, dear friends, dear,
Where blooms of laughter linger near.
In the fragrant threads of joy we weave,
The scented memories never leave.

## **Lullaby for Lost Blossoms**


In twilight's hush, the blooms still sway,
A lullaby for those who play.
With fading hues and sleepy yawn,
The petals sigh, their night reborn.

The flowers hum a gentle tune,
As shadows dance, they're over the moon.
A marigold slips, its petals wide,
Into a slumber, they blissfully glide.

With whispers soft as twilight's grace,
They share their dreams, each petal's place.
A story spun from starry light,
For wayward blooms that say goodnight.

So close your eyes and dream along,
As flowers weave their close-out song.
In the garden's heart, they find their rest,
A lullaby by the blossoms blessed.

## Beneath the Blooming Sky

Under arches of white blooms, we sway,
Dancing in dreams where bees love to play.
The fragrance calls, brings a tickle to nose,
As laughter erupts with each gust that blows.

A picnic's laid, but where's the sweet bread?
The ants threw a party, we weren't misled.
Friends dressed as flowers, oh what a sight!
Silly hats worn, feelings take flight.

Sipping our drinks, a splash made its mark,
A bee found our picnic, and left quite a spark.
Chasing our snacks, it buzzed with delight,
Who knew a small insect could cause such a fright?

Days under blossoms make for silly tales,
Creating memories that no one derails.
So here's to the laughter, the fun we define,
Beneath the sky blooming, we found joy divine.

## The Tenderness of Yesterdays

Time slips away like a breeze through the trees,
It tickles the past, brings a smile, a tease.
We chase after moments, as they slip by fast,
Those days filled with blooms, how lovely they passed.

We wore silly hats, adorned with the cheer,
Laughed through the evening, with friends always near.
The sun dipped low as we danced through the haze,
In sweetness of memory, we savor our days.

Once we tried making a potion of bliss,
A mix of those blossoms and sweet lemon twist.
But nature had plans that went wildly astray,
The neighbors still chuckle at what went their way.

Yet here's to the past, those delightful yesterdays,
Where laughter and flowers colored our ways.
With each little stumble, our hearts took the lead,
In tenderness wrapped, we planted the seed.

## Whispers of Blossoms

Whispers of petals float soft on the breeze,
They giggle and chatter, with insistent tease.
"Join us," they beckon, "in joy, set the stage,
Turn frowns into laughter, let's break out of cage!"

Sipping on nectar, a very fine brew,
A hint of sweet mischief is breathed in anew.
Flowers conspiring as pollen takes flight,
Raising a ruckus from morning till night.

With birds weaving songs, they join in the fun,
A symphony rises, we dance, one by one.
"Who needs a dance floor? Just take to the grass,
In this wild garden, let laughter amass!"

So let's paint the world with our vibrant cheer,
With whispers of blossoms, we keep laughter near.
For each petal that falls holds a story untold,
A lesson in joy, in humor it's bold.

## The Last Petal's Muse

The last petal falls with a flip and a twirl,
It lands in a giggle, a bright little whirl.
Just when I thought it was all said and done,
It winks as it lands, oh what a small fun!

Gather up petals, we weave them in chains,
A crown for a jester who dances in lanes.
With tipsy old fairies who spill all their tea,
In shadows of laughter, they giggle with glee.

Who knew such a bloom held so much delight?
Each whisper, each chuckle, turns day into night.
The garden is bursting with stories to share,
With laughter so bright, we've quite the affair!

So let's toast the petals that flutter and sway,
To laughter and joy in the bloom of the day.
For each light-hearted moment, each giggle that stews,
We find in each petal, the last petal's muse.

## Beneath the Blooms of Yesteryear

Once in the garden, time flew fast,
Dancing with petals, a shadow cast.
Bumblebees giggled, the sun wore a grin,
As whispers of flavors, invited us in.

Lemonade dreams, we sipped in glee,
With sprigs of laughter as wild as the sea.
Under the arch of sweet fragrance delight,
We tripped over roots in the soft golden light.

The cats wore hats—it was quite the show,
With daisies in tails, they strutted their flow.
A raccoon with style, in a vest, quite profound,
Beneath old blooms where joy was unbound.

## The Unfolding Silence

In the quiet moments, laughter would bloom,
As trees told tales of once lively rooms.
A rogue squirrel plotting, with nutty finesse,
In a world draped in foliage, it's chaos, no less.

Whispers of blossoms, like giggles in spring,
You'd swear the wind had a penchant for zing.
'Twas a time when the owls wore tuxedos at night,
And danced with the fireflies in shimmering flight.

The hives of bees held debates on their flair,
While butterflies chuckled at all the fanfare.
Under moonlit laughter, the silliness soared,
In gardens of yore where joy was adored.

## Chronicles of the Forgotten Grove

In a grove where the past wore a humorous grin,
The trees shared secrets, and squirrels chimed in.
Their gossiping leaves, like a well-timed joke,
With fables and farces through twirls of oak.

A wise old hedgehog with spectacles perched,
Lectured the flowers—oh how they lurched!
With petals a-flutter, they giggled and spun,
In a waltz with the breeze, oh what fun had begun!

A picnic of stories, with laughter as bread,
The ants served their acorns, as joys spread ahead.
Each tale in the grove, like a ticklish breeze,
Churned chuckles and grins with the greatest of ease.

## A Twilight Reverie

When shadows grew long in the fading light,
The world wore a smile, things felt just right.
Fireflies hosting a sparkly ball,
Where daisies donned crowns, standing proud and tall.

The moon, a jester, played tricks with the stars,
Juggling with crickets, striking whimsical bars.
As laughter echoed through branches entwined,
In twilight, a sense of pure fun was designed.

With petals in pockets, adventures unfold,
Mischief and mirth brought warmth against cold.
A riddle of joy for the night to embrace,
In the heart of the grove, life was a warm place.

# Petals Kissed by Time

Petals dancing in the breeze,
Wobbling like they're at the knees.
Each glance a wink from the past,
Time flies, but blooms hold steadfast.

Bees polka with the pollen,
While grannies tell tales, often fallen.
Giggles echo through the glade,
As blossoms join in the charade.

Fuzzy memories waving 'hello',
In garden parties where laughter flows.
Grown-ups can't dance like they did,
But beads of joy cannot be hid.

Time's a jester with a crown,
Yet here the silly blooms won't frown.
Each petal's tale is a laugh,
As we sip sweet tea, the half and half.

## The Shade of Nostalgia

Underneath the wobbly boughs,
Time passes, yet who cares, wow!
Leaves gossip in a breezy hush,
As memories make us blush.

Sipping juice from frosted cups,
Swapping stories, hiccups and ups.
Grandma's hat flies high and wild,
As laughter's echo fills the mild.

The flowers nod with knowing grins,
As we reminisce where we've been.
Time trickles like a honey stream,
Each moment is a giggling dream.

Shadows dance like silly sprites,
And we're lost in pastel lights.
Party hats on blooms or ferns,
In this shade, the world still turns.

## Beneath the Canopy of Memories

Under vast canopies above,
Laughter fits like a favorite glove.
Old tales twist with the sunny rays,
While petal-dancers steal the gaze.

Forget-me-nots tease time's flow,
In corners where joy starts to grow.
With each sip of lemonade,
Urgent stories start to cascade.

Bees are buzzing a mellow tune,
While blooms sway softly, afternoon.
In this merry, fragrant scene,
We twirl and sway, where joy's the queen.

Through tangled thoughts and wild delights,
We chase the sun on dreamy flights.
A buttercup gives me a wink,
As we all gather for a drink.

## **Blooming Into Silence**

In the garden where giggles freeze,
Blooms bloom loud, but hum with ease.
Whispers of petals, soft and sweet,
As silence dances, light on feet.

Each fragrant petal holds a jest,
As time pauses for a rest.
Memories sprout in the sun,
While shadows chuckle, 'This is fun!'

When laughter fades, it's not all lost,
In petals' memory, we find the cost.
Sipping shadows, we share our laughs,
With colorful stories on leafy halves.

The quiet blooms bring joy again,
As petals dance where hearts have been.
And in this stillness, we rejoice,
In every silent, blooming voice.

## Echoes in the Garden

In a garden lush and quaint,
The flowers whisper tales and paint.
Bees buzz around with silly cheer,
Cracking jokes we cannot hear.

A bunny munches on a leaf,
Wearing spectacles—a funny chief.
The gnomes chuckle, oh what a sight,
As clouds do dance in playful flight.

Petals rain down like confetti,
As squirrels prance, all bright and petty.
With every fresh breeze, laughter flows,
In this garden, joy overflows.

The sun grins wide, the daisies sway,
In this floral cabaret of play.
With every bloom, a joke is spun,
Life's comedy has just begun.

## The Last Dance of the Blossom

When spring bids us a cheeky farewell,
A final dance, do flowers tell.
They twirl and swirl on petals soft,
While bees joke and tumble aloft.

A dandelion's wig is askew,
It's the highlight of this floral view.
The daisies giggle in the breeze,
And even thorns manage to tease.

As petals fall, a wink is shared,
With laughter sweet, all hearts are bared.
The sun bows down, a jester proud,
While flowers party, drawing a crowd.

So let the last petal drift away,
In this bonkers bouquet ballet.
For every goodbye, there's a laugh,
In nature's whimsical, wild path.

# Fragments of a Sweet Goodbye

A breeze carries stories, light and spry,
While blossoms giggle, a farewell sigh.
With every sway, they tease and play,
    Sharing secrets from yesterday.

The last blooms cheer, in riotous glee,
Practicing lines for their next jubilee.
A fading petal winks, and then--
It's a punchline, again and again!

The grass beneath offers hearty laughs,
    While ants march on in floral paths.
With one last shimmy, the petals part,
    Leaving behind a chuckling heart.

So when you wander where flowers reside,
    Remember the giggles in every stride.
Each fragment whispers, 'Goodbye for now!'
A sweet jest from the earth's blooming brow.

## Boughs Bowed with Memory

Boughs bend low, with stories to tell,
In a woodland warm, where laughter fell.
Branches schemed with whimsical glee,
Holding memories like a jubilee.

Old trees chuckle, their leaves all aglow,
As critters converse in a breezy show.
With every rustle, a chuckle goes by,
As squirrels reenact the best woodland spy.

Laughter echoes, a sweet serenade,
From every bloom in the soft parade.
With petals swirling like ribbons in flight,
Each moment captured in joy's delight.

So dance, you blooms, beneath skies so blue,
In this garden's glee, where fun feels true.
For boughs bowed down with memories sweet,
Make every goodbye a hilarious treat.

# Forgotten Garden Dreams

In a garden where weeds hold sway,
The daisies have thrown a grand soiree.
The gnomes are all tipsy, quite absurd,
And the roses are gossiping, what a word!

The herbs are plotting their herbivore fight,
As oregano shimmies, quite a sight!
The tulips are tumbling, laughing anew,
While violets are singing, oh what a crew!

Brought together by a whimsical breeze,
Vegetables join in, shaking their knees.
Zucchini, once shy, now takes the stage,
In a dance that would make even onions gauge!

So here's to the garden where dreams abound,
Where mischief and laughter can always be found.
In this wild patch of joy, 'neath the sun's beam,
We toast to the flowers of forgotten dreams!

## When Flowers Fade

When blossoms bow out, with a sigh and a dance,
The petals left behind take a chance.
They gossip and chuckle, with humor so sly,
Pretending they've left, oh my, oh my!

The sunflowers grumble, their faces so wide,
As lilies lament with their petals in stride.
The daffodils chuckle, mark their own fate,
While violets roll on, not caring, just great!

The bees reminisce of sweet nectar days,
How they danced with a blossom in summer's rays.
But now as the leaves start to crinkle and fade,
The flowers laugh on, in this grand charade!

So fear not the fading, it's all just a show,
The garden's a stage where the wildflowers grow.
With humor unmasked, and laughter we trade,
For every bloom's end a new jest is made!

# The Weaving of a Wind's Whisper

Through the trees, the whispers come dancing by,
Like gossiping birds, painting the sky.
They twirl with the daisies, oh what a sight,
While the butterflies argue who's dazzling and bright!

The breeze weaves a yarn, a tale to be told,
Of blossoms who giggle, both daring and bold.
The dandelions puff, their wisdom so grand,
Sowing seeds of mischief all over the land!

As the tulips stand guard, in their colors so bold,
They keep out the snails, with their tales made of gold.
Each petal's a story, a quirk of the breeze,
In their woven world, there's always a tease!

So listen, dear friend, with an ear open wide,
To the whispers of nature, where giggles abide.
For life's but a tapestry spun from our play,
With flowers and laughter to brighten the way!

## **A Solitary Blossom's Hymn**

In a field all alone, a lone bloom stands tall,
With a top hat and cane, it's the life of the ball.
It sways and it bows, with a chuckle and twirl,
Singing songs of delight, making all nature whirl!

The bees stop to gawk, their work left undone,
While the nearby trees join in, having fun.
"I'll show you the moves," the blossom declares,
As it boogies and winks, without any cares!

The grass looks on green, quite envious yet,
For this solo performer has no need to fret.
With petals ablaze in the late afternoon,
It dances and laughs, like a merry little tune!

So here's to the brave, the solitary sprout,
Who knows how to dance, despite the doubt.
It sings to the heavens, loud and clear,
For a flower that laughs, has no reason to fear!

## A Tribute to the Bloom

Oh flower so bright, in dress so white,
You dance with the breeze, a whimsical sight.
Your scent fills the air, sweet like a tease,
Spreading laughter and joy, with effortless ease.

In gardens you spread, a jolly brigade,
With bees as your fans, in nature's parade.
You frolic with buds, in a silly spree,
Bringing smiles all round, just look and you'll see.

But alas, dear bloom, it's time to depart,
So we gather 'round, with cake and a tart.
We'll toast to your life, with cups all a-clink,
And dance one last jig, before we all sink.

Oh, how we shall miss the jokes that you told,
In whispers of wind, and petals of gold.
So here's to you, friend, in laughter we bask,
Forever remembered, and that's the last task!

## The Vanishing Heritage

Once in the meadows, you ruled with flair,
A crown of pure white, with fragrance to share.
But whispers of change, oh what a distress,
In silence you fade, we must all confess.

The bees don't arrive, their buzz lost in tune,
Gone like the socks that vanish at noon.
We search high and low, in hedges and glen,
Only to find socks, never your pen.

So here's to the days when your blooms filled the sky,
With laughter and giggles, oh my, oh my!
Yet today we proclaim, with a chuckle and sigh,
"Dear heritage lost, but we'll still say hi!"

For though you diminish, we'll keep up the fun,
With stories of you, still shining like sun.
A laugh with each petal, a memory bright,
Dear flower, we miss you, yet hold you so tight!

## **Fleeting Moments in Floral**

In gardens you giggled, with petals so grand,
Twirling and whirling, a bold little band.
Your joy is infectious, like a bright sunny chat,
But blink and it's gone, just like that, just like that!

You pop up in spring, with a wink and a nod,
Leaving us dazed, like a poor little cod.
We laughed 'til we cried, as you danced in the sun,
Now we muse on your charm, now that you're done.

The fleeting of blooms, oh how they confound,
Like socks in the dryer, never to be found!
But we'll raise a glass, to the fun that you gave,
A toast to the laughter, you brought to this rave!

So float on, dear flower, wherever you roam,
In memories' garden, you've found a sweet home.
With smiles and some giggles, you'll never depart,
For you live in our laughter, and deep in our heart!

## Sorrow of the Sunlit Grove

In the sunlit grove, a flower would grin,
With petals unfurling, like a wild violin.
We'd laugh at the bees, their clumsy ballet,
Yet now they seem lost, the companionship frayed.

Each moment was captured in fragrance and fun,
But alas, gentle bloom, you've decided to run.
We'll miss that sweet chuckle that bloomed through the air,
While sharing our secrets, with hardly a care.

As shadows grow long, we sigh with delight,
For all of your antics, oh they were a sight!
Yet sadness creeps in, as the petals drift down,
With a wink of a leaf, you've left us to frown.

So here in this grove, where light used to play,
We'll gather your laughter to keep shadows at bay.
And as we reminisce, we'll wear smiles so wide,
For in our fond hearts, you forever abide!

www.ingramcontent.com/pod-product-compliance
Lightning Source LLC
Chambersburg PA
CBHW071815160426
43209CB00003B/92